Count and Save with Blue

Published by Advance Publishers, L.C.
www.advance-publishers.com

©2000 Viacom International Inc. All rights reserved. Nickelodeon,
Blue's Clues and all related titles, logos and characters are trademarks
of Viacom International Inc.
Visit Blue's Clues online at www.nickjr.com

Written by K. Emily Hutta
Art layout by Niall Harding
Art composition by sheena needham • ess design
Produced by Bumpy Slide Books

ISBN: 1-57973-083-3

Blue's Clues Discovery Series

Hi! We're glad to see you. Blue wants to buy a birthday present for Magenta, but she doesn't know if she has enough money. She needs twelve Blue dollars for the present. Will you help us count Blue's money? You will? Great! So how many Blue dollars does Blue have? Yeah, four Blue dollars. You are so smart!

But wait . . . Blue needs twelve Blue dollars for Magenta's gift. What is it you want to buy for her, Blue?

Oh, okay. We'll play Blue's Clues to figure out what present Blue wants to buy for Magenta. Will you help me? Great!

Hi, Steve. Hi, Blue. How are you doing today?

Hi, Mr. Salt and Mrs. Pepper. Blue wants to buy a special birthday present for Magenta, but she doesn't have enough money.

Why don't you have a ke sale to earn more money, Blue? We'll help you.

A bake sale! What a great idea! Can we make cookies to sell?

Yes, and we can make muffins, too.

Let's gather together the eight ingredients for the muffins.

Let's see. Do we have everything we need for the muffins?
BROWN SUGAR

Uh . . . there are supposed to be eight ingredients. But there are . . . how many are there? Right. Six! So I guess that means we are missing . . . yeah, two. We're missing two ingredients.

Here are the two missing ingredients, eggs and vanilla.
Now we need twelve muffin cups in the muffin pans.

Twelve. Okay. Nothing to it. But wait . . . twelve is a lot. Do we have enough muffin cups to fill up the pans? We do? Cool!

The muffins are baking, so now it's time to make cookies. We've already mixed the ingredients together. Now let's see how many we can make.

How many more cookies do you think we can fit on this cookie sheet? Yeah, three. I think so, too.

These are going to be some delicious cookies! Now that the dough is on the cookie sheets, what should we do next? Yeah! Put them in the oven!

Hey, the cookies and muffins are done. We'd better get set up for our bake sale so Blue can make money to buy her present for Magenta!

Oh, you see a clue? It's a tail. A tail is our first clue! Hmmm. I think we need to find two more clues.

Wow! The cookies and muffins are selling fast. I wonder how many we have left. Good idea! Let's count them!

Hey, I'd better get a cookie before they're all gone!

You see a clue? It's the color pink—that's our second clue! So what could Blue want to buy Magenta that has a tail and is the color pink? Yeah, I think we need to find our last clue.

Wow, look at all of these Blue dollars
Blue earned at the bake sale! Do you think
she made enough to buy Magenta's present?
Yeah! We'll count all the Blue dollars.

Let's see . . . Blue made eight dollars at the bake sale, and she already had four Blue dollars to start with. So that makes . . . yeah! Twelve dollars! You are so smart! Hey! Do you know what that means? Blue has enough money to buy a present for Magenta!

Our bake sale was a huge success!
What's that? A clue? Oh, on the Blue dollar!
So money is our last clue! You know what that
means, don't you? It's time to go to our . . .
Thinking Chair!

So our three clues are a tail, the color pink, and money. Hmmm. What present could Blue want to buy Magenta?

You may be right! Let's ask Blue.

Hey, Blue! Is your birthday present for Magenta a piggy bank? It is? All right! We just figured out Blue's Clues!

It looks like Magenta loves her new piggy bank. Now Magenta has a place to save her money! Thanks for your help solving Blue's Clues. 'Bye!

"SAVE WITH BLUE" PIGGY BANK

You will need: a plastic 1-liter bottle and cap, a pink sponge, pink felt, 2 matching buttons, a pink pipe cleaner, a craft knife (just for grown-ups), and craft glue

1. Ask a grown-up to cut a pink sponge into circles for the feet, glue them in place, and hold with tape until set.

2. Ask a grown-up to help you cut two 3-inch-wide triangles of pink felt. Fold the triangles in half and glue the lower edges together (use a paper clip to hold them together until they're dry). Trim the ears into ear shapes and glue them to the bottle.

3. Glue on the buttons to make eyes.

4. Ask a grown-up to use the craft knife to make a small hole in the bottle for the pipe cleaner tail and a slot in the top to drop your coins in!